Letters
from the
Periphery

Also by Alex Skovron

Poetry

The Rearrangement (1988)
Sleeve Notes (1992)
Infinite City: 100 Sonnetinas (1999)
Chess and other poems (chapbook, 2002)
The Man and the Map (2003)
Autographs: 56 poems in prose (2008)
Towards the Equator: New & Selected Poems (2014)

Fiction

The Poet: a novella (2005)
The Man who Took to his Bed (stories, 2017)

In translation

The Attic (French bilingual: trans. Jacques Rancourt, 2013)
Water Music (Chinese bilingual: trans. Xu Daozhi, 2017)

The Poet and *The Man who Took to his Bed*
(both in Czech: trans. Josef Tomáš and Hana Tomková, 2014, 2019)

Audio

Towards the Equator (CD: author reading from his poetry, 2019)

As Editor

The Concise Encyclopaedia of Australia (General Editor, 1979)
Singing for All He's Worth (with Raimond Gaita and Alex Miller, 2011)

Letters
from the
Periphery

Alex Skovron

PUNCHER & WATTMANN

First published in 2021, reprinted 2022, 2024
Published by Puncher & Wattmann
PO Box 441
Glebe NSW 2037

http://www.puncherandwattmann.com
puncherandwattmann@bigpond.com

A catalogue record for this
book is available from the
National Library of Australia

Skovron, Alex
Letters from the Periphery
ISBN   9781925780833

Cover design by Miranda Douglas
(inspired by Grace Crowley, *Abstract painting*, 1952)

Text in Adobe Garamond Pro 11/14.8
Printed by Lightning Source International

This project has been assisted by the Australian Government through the Australia Council, its arts funding and advisory body.

Australian Government

Australia Council
for the Arts

for
Lennon and Zephyr

Avi & Pauline
Shani, Tamar & Shilo, Lee-Ronn & Sha

and in memory of Gita

Contents

'Arriving at each new city, the traveller finds again
a past of his that he did not know he had …'

— Italo Calvino, *Invisible Cities*

On the Beach

'Our dreams have their anchor
In the burning ember, deep,
By the chambers of the sea.'
  — Czesław Miłosz, 'A Family'

The boats are rearranged along the shore,
smoke trickles absently from hazy roofs
shadowed by clouds and the declining day.
No moon. Just rustle of insistent waves
that rummage back and forth among the grey
sand and the seaweed rendering the slope
up onto the embankment. Two shapes there
unframed against the sky stand motionless,
until one lifts an arm to the other's waist
and they walk off into the northern gloom.
The masts creak in the unassuming breeze,
shuffle and nudge as if in gentle contest
for some advantage ships alone can know,
and planks that glisten in the moonless sheen
of evening, and the severed wind,
measure out the jetty's slanting deck,
await what visitors the dawn will bring
or not. And as we watch, the lonely duo
have appeared again, reclining inexplicably
beside the blade of a primordial rock
whose outline darkens as the sky moves on.
And so do they. Shortly they drift along
and vanish past the headland to the south:
and we are left to ask each other's eyes
if we should follow in their wake or stay
for the duration of the night, the week, the world.

The Wedge

We scouted among the ruins
that had been the Monastery, confessing
unease when we suddenly noticed
we were treading on the graves of monks
who had lain at peace beneath us
(perhaps at peace) since the Black Death.

At vespers, as we nestled into a wedge
in the west wing of the chapel, its walls
now ghostly remnants of moss-covered stone,
you pointed to a derelict well still intact
on the open, once-cobbled courtyard.

A solitary vulture (so my fancy had it)
perched on the crank shaped like a squared Z
and studied us with what you deemed
a 'suspicious malice', averting your eyes.

I flung an arm into the air, back and forth,
to startle the creature, but it merely sat,
fastidiously revising now and then
its clawhold on the weatherbeaten wood.

Then came the cloudburst, and the bird
took hefty flight, careful to encircle us
six times (I had to count), right above our niche,
before lifting into the despondent sky
with a lean shriek, barely a backward glance.

Visitation

At one point, exhausted from pilgrimage,
we ceased exploring the drowsy churchyard
because I wanted a photograph of you
standing at the centre of the ruined transept
of this relic from the Wars of the Roses;
but just as the shutter clicked, you squinted
toward the skyline, disturbed by a muted drone
that became a glinting speck high in the west
and shimmered into a flying machine—one
of those biplanes we could both remember
from before the war, one very like a Tiger Moth
father had hoisted me onto somewhere
deep among the lost paddocks of the past,
deep among all the dimmed remembrances
of a childhood whose measure had been flight,
from one home, one school to the next,
in pursuit of a future we never found; and here,
now, this visitation, and I began to reimagine
that summer's day, an old barn burning
beside the airfield, my first ice-cream, father
handing me gently into the tall cockpit
I had so yearned to conquer, mother, unsure,
hovering on the periphery … But as I drifted
aboard the memory of that morning, the plane,
by now almost exactly at our zenith,
gave out a choking stutter, stalled, and plunged,
in a silent beautiful spiral, into a copse
on the far side of the ridge above the church;
you clamped a palm to your mouth, but I
could only stare as the plume crawled upward,
heavenward, black as an afterthought.

Ghost Trains

I had mentioned my fascination with railways
as we fossicked between corroded tracks
treading time along the overgrown platform
that had landed no locomotive since the war.
The glance you gave just then made me suspect
you shared no such attraction, intent rather
on the flora splashed outside the old station-house
and into the distance on the slopes and ripples
that spread their wares ahead of the lilac hills
to the west. Yet a minute later you found my hand,
pressed, whispered something I couldn't make out,
and I suddenly noticed the tear on your cheek
and the slight blush, and our afternoon dispersed
because you were weeping softly into yourself.
So when I paused there with you in the middle
of the empty siding above those coppery rails
and eroded sleepers like some haphazard fallen
stepladder stretched into the horizon, and took
your other hand and turned you toward me to ask
why you were unhappy, you simply reached
into the pockets of my army-disposal greatcoat
and slumped against me, into me, until our chins
settled on one another's shoulder and my arms
had to encircle you and we stood for the first time
as one, and I heard you draw a quivering breath
and whisper, again, the words that had escaped me.

Compulsion

Because one July, as the armies stood off
    along the disputed river, while I,
adrift in our ridiculous farmhouse, struggled
    to finesse the closing lines
of a verse that was refusing to collaborate,
    you turned from the oaken bench
that divided our makeshift kitchen,
    a black olive tweezered in your fingers,
and, alert to my relentless dismay
    over the fragment I'd just read to you,
softly proposed: 'You must change
    your pathetic antagonism to this war.'
I dropped my pen, stood upright,
    reached across the bench to steal
a kalamata from the jar, then slipped outside
    and made a dash for the moors,
despite the warnings by the Home Guard
    of mines and unspent munitions.
I raced on, right out to the little pinewood,
    past the clearing where we'd
exchanged our once undying devotions,
    and, surprising myself, swung
onto the renegade branch of a rustling oak
    generations ancient; and there,
cupping my furrowed palms to my mouth
    I shouted a string of imprecations
in a language I had never heard,
    then subsided to the earth, slumped
against the all-forgiving trunk, wept
    into the future of my tormented land.

Disputation

'How many kingdoms know nothing of us!'
— Pascal, *Pensées*

In those years we could still remember the future.
Every day we'd stroll the broken arcades
and cloisters of the Academy; so often
the abbot seemed on the point of speaking, lips ajar,
but seldom words. From no clear cause
he would produce his tattered breviary, and pressed
within were those little pieces of the past
he had not stopped worshipping, all yellowed now
from the devotions of the sun. Occasionally
he'd succumb to an attack of enthusiasm and the world
became salvageable again; yet he quickly
bristled if I should hazard (say) to invoke Loyola,
suggest that laughter alone could redeem *our* world,
a kingdom lost and perplexed. To which
his inner Benedict would leap up in refutation
(Chapter 7, Rule 10), point heavenward, and declare:
'Come forth and set the world on fire!'
Once, when I adverted primly to my Spaniard's creed
—'Act as if everything depended on you'—
he flashed his smug beatific sneer and converted:
'But trust as if everything depends on God!'
speciously whispering into my cheek that after all
Ignatius was only human. At such times
the afternoon would come down like a penance.
The milling scholars, black-robed and pale as rubricators,
shadowed each other among the Ionic colonnades,
disregarding the airships that circled the slowing sky
or stood off among the ingenuous clouds,
proclaiming their terrible heresy.

Four Last Things

'already the air grows dark …'
— Joseph von Eichendorff

These were the last things.
A breeze from somewhere making the leaves
of the calendar fan out, and then subside.
The spire of St Lucian on the corso,
transfixing the balcony wall with a needle
of light kindled on its gilded crucifix.
One motorcycle in the street below,
its pilot yelling at the unruly mob
of sheep traversing; and the locomotive,
stagnant within its girders; and three burly
foot-soldiers abusing the tattered
herdsman—they reel from a drunk symposium
and grimace in glee, each to the other,
over the hapless wench they had arraigned
(officially at first) then shared into the dawn;
their whips swish at the shepherd,
the train gives out a sympathetic hiss,
a sparrow fossicks in the dust. And then
the very last—a threnody uncurls
from an upper window hollowed by a burst
of misdirected gunfire yesterday,
a shadowy contralto, luscious, terrible,
trailing away into the reddened sky.

Only the Music

Each cloud contains the history of the world.
If you gaze long enough into the eye of the moon
    you will guess the truth of creation. Do not stare
    into the sun, for you will be blinded with brilliant
half-truths, dazzling mirages that you will carry
like a false faith for all the rest of your days.
    Be on guard against the wind, it carries the seeds
    of the death of each civilization, even your own,
and the implosion of your belief will leave you lame,
prone to promptings of the divine, a boulder you will
    unearth, upend, to discover the crawling cosmos
    beneath. Always respect the word of birds, who
know everything but sing riddles with eloquent wings.
Above all, be vigilant of those about you who would
    offer you the language of the sky, would deafen
    your soul for one sip of infinity, would lead
you into the labyrinths of becoming—the canals
of those regions where no water flows, only tears
    and ancient blood; where the stone strata rise up
    into limitless black, descend in dizzy spirals
deep below the circles of the underworld. I tell you
this in confidence, knowing that you will forget.
    Go now, and remember only the music concealed
    behind the illusion that you know yourself.

Mickey Mouse Club

I saw them kiss next to the televisions—I mean
just outside, on the footpath. It was the 1950s,
the stores all up and down Oxford Street, well,
Grace Brothers for sure, had TVs on display,
and I spotted them *necking* (that was the word
then) up against the plate-glass window once,
in the middle of *Disneyland* or *Wagon Train*.

Every day, it seemed, there was more to see,
but my cousin Vince reckoned that best of all
he liked 'Test Pattern and Music' (that's what
was listed in our *TV Times*, right after 'Close'),
but since he wasn't allowed to stay up late
he would trot down to the local electrical shop
of a morning, before the start of transmission,
press his face inward expectantly till the glass
fogged up. Lucy for her part, usually with him,
would skip across the street to the dressmaker's
opposite, to gape again at the dummy bride
becalmed in her lacy but headless splendour,
a chip below her knee that only I knew about.

What *did* we know then of, well, anything?
I tried to avoid them, with their Fantasyland
tele-romance, keener on the swings and slide
behind the post office, satisfied some evenings
after school to knock on the Aberdeens' door,
three houses down from our flat, and settle
on the carpet with their Gary and little Rosalie
in front of *The Mickey Mouse Club*, looking out
for Darlene or Cheryl or whatever-her-name,
lusting after them in my ten-year-old way,
while Mr and Mrs A. stood in their kitchen
behind us, *smooching*—like in those movies
at the Star we weren't supposed to be allowed into.

Around the World

'Like a medieval Latvian serf I wait
For something to wait for.'
    — Mikelis Norgelis (Michael O'Loughlin, *In This Life*)

Sydney, sixteen and a half, I took part
in a chess tournament called the Riga Shield,
knowing nothing then of that fabled city.
Byzantium too was yet to traverse my page,
like poetry, and Prague remained
a station where we'd waited eight years ago,
in a wagon from Warsaw to Vienna,
for something that would arrive soon enough—
my first climb above the gorgeous clouds
of the Mediterranean behind a Convair
cabin window, front row, portside, right behind
the flight deck's forbidden musics.
I did know something of the Baltic states
(Soviet Republics then), from *Around the World*:
some of its pictures brought me the shock
of the real, especially the chapterette 'IRAN'—
brown print of two blindfolded figures
each strung slumped to a pole, labelled ın Polish
'Bestial execution of democrats sentenced
by the shah's regime'. It sat opposite
a sample stamp and the silhouetted little map
of the country in question dark within its diagram
continent. I treasure that book, although
now of course I know: little changes—
in some places you can hang for mixing metaphors.
I was happy to mix chess with geography, both
I grew to love. They somehow seemed
to complement each other—and me, in my
consequential otherness. These days we're cajoled
into splitting our differences, it wasn't always
thus. But as I edged into 1965, newer skies

unfolding before me, sixteen and a half, that chess
of becoming (my games all zealously notated),
I too was balancing the difference—
between where I had been or never been,
and whatever I couldn't know I was waiting for.

Double Clock

Our backyard, concreted over,
was turned into a chessboard,
crimson and yellow, painted
by my father with slide-rule
exactitude, metre by metre,
each square a metre square,
though this was the mid-sixties
and yards were stepped-out in
yards. He had to work around
the Hills Hoist, of course,
and over the disconcertingly
less-than-level cementwork,
with its tiny pocks and glitches
subverting the subtlety of
his craft. I was learning things,
having bought on impulse
Fred Reinfeld's little *Chess
in a Nutshell* (Permabooks,
1958) at our '63 school fête,
quickly becoming hooked. Soon
I'd be climbing Moore Street,
steep as the Dickson Park slide,
to dash along Bondi Road
with my virginal shaves, my
Old Spice, and my sharp new
black pullover, so urbane.
Those Tuesday evenings
upstairs at the chess club
in the School of Arts were my
wondrous early tilt towards
a fresh selfdom—like the buses
I'd board soon for the YWCA
where the city club sat,

where I would sit pounding
the double clock, an eye often
elsewhere. And marching home
from the 380 or '81 down
Wellington Street, the slippery-
dip of Moore, I could peer over
into our unduplicable domain
and make out the pattern
in the dark, and my mother too,
her window silhouette, anxious
already that I hadn't returned …
And after fifty-odd years,
with dad and mum long gone
from Edward Street, I fancy
that magic grid, all red and gold,
still chessing the yard, faded yes,
but undisturbed, having earned
each new owner's new accord.
In truth it must be impossible
to erase, without excavating
all that I've buried there.

Carousel Days

And one evening, constellating the dots
from the top deck of Civil Engineering
my gaze skimmed beyond Delta Orionis
and I suddenly detected a tiny shifting

of the sky's slant, an opening that said—
look hard enough into us drizzling stars
and you will discover more of yourself
than if you drank from an endless chalice

of the choicest rum. And I forgot about
the fragrant maiden, eighteen, next to me
(myself only just crossing twenty), forgot
the spring night's rooftop seminar, transit

of the morning star, all the lecture notes
foldered in my bag, the poems fattening
my little black book with the bright red
spine, and I stared like some ridiculously

transported thing, a boy who'd disturbed
for a mere moment and twisted some key,
glimpsing a doorway to a language meant
(he was certain) for him alone. And each

waking minute in carousel days to come
he would search to regain it, to translate
what, upon that starstruck roof, had stung
his soul. He is there still, translating it yet.

From the Thirteenth Floor

Cambridge Hotel, Sydney

Dawn dims the safelight of the moon
      as day dissolves
      into itself in the sky's tray

An aeroplane is crawling heavily
      between one spire
      and the next, and the next
      moment has vanished
      like all moments into the next

Time attempts to cling onto itself but
      there is nothing there
      the minutes on the radio-clock
      blink out their hoax

Even the inflected silence is counterfeit
      its undertow swept
      with the audible detritus
      of antisilence, the hum
      of the enclosing certainties

But a window-cleaner abseiling down
      the semi-glassed façade
      of a neighbouring tower
      like film unspooling

Distracts: a man, bare-chested, sprawled
      across a couch
      in a room on a line with mine
      is twiddling a remote
      to learn what he surely knows

The shadows flow, forge their habitual
        shapings, they fix
        the city with itinerant light
        to blacken or glaze
        each stroke and surface
        of the mapmaker's design

Morning has assembled its demands
        another plane slits
        the clouds' membrane
        an electric drill is juddering
        from the suite next door
        the curtains stir, restless for
        unavailable breeze

I slide my thoughts out gently, clip them
        like dripping prints
        to the crowded cord that sways
        in the glowing dark
        just there behind my eyes

Climate Change

'We have no control over the past. There are as many
secrets in it as in the future.'

— Adam Zagajewski, *Two Cities*

The past never happened and never will
the future has come and gone
the present is loitering somewhere on the outskirts
of intention, biding its time, alone

among the old tenses with no place to turn
and nothing to do but await
word from the foggy reaches of instamatic memory
as it scans itself, recalling too late

the long latitudes of desire, all those isobars
swimming about an erratic map
like an eternally changing and unchartable weather
like crosshairs that refuse to overlap

to fix at last upon their softly shining target
lurking somewhere in the zone
of a past that no longer can pretend to happen
and a future forever gone.

Arcane Geometry

'Where is the truth of unremembered things?'
— Czesław Miłosz, 'The Separate Notebooks'

It is the unremembered things which harbour truth;
    things forgotten and things pushed past forgetting,
that surface suddenly in the creak of a gate
    at sunset, or jolt us out of a dream of forbidden cellars
where our first kiss went untasted, rooms
    where we whispered nothing and the night alone
witnessed the contours of our febrile silence.
    Admit that the hazy outline of the staircase down into
the deep decades is beyond your grasp,
    it quivers there, just across the chasm of a thought;
confess that no truer note calls from the gone seasons
    than that pulse of longing somewhere so near, almost
audible—behind, within—each time you cross
    the open quadrangles and shadowed cloisters that turn
your imaginings into daguerreotypes
    of unrequited fancy, warm velleities or cooling hopes
that refuse to surrender their essence which is
    your essence. How often has a song requickened
from a car radio ancient pleasures abandoned or unknown,
    or carved abruptly a channel into childhood's
helpless diligence, transforming the moment
    into a truth that is yet impossible to reshape
into the touchable, a clue from some arcane geometry
    whose angles you cannot decipher no matter how you
strain to translate its axioms into legible script?
    Where, then, is that which, long dead, is yet alive
but irrecallable, barely glimpsed, forever blanketed
    under the fathomless cloak of the past? And when
will there come a chance to snatch at that cloak,
    expose the outlines and contours of the elusive psalm
beneath?—To confront at last the true trace of time,
    the unremembered things that wait quietly

inside the dusty almanacs of our desires?—To strip away
    the illusions we employ a lifetime to tend and cultivate
while the truths we do remember wither in the hothouse
    we inhabit?—To reveal the forgotten garden
that flourishes somewhere there, among the shaded beds
    and hidden furrows of what we mistake for ourselves?

To My Half-Brother

i.m. Aleksander Skowron (1942–1944)

You'd be just about seventy by now.
I imagine you walking through the door,
to announce, 'Hello, I'm here, your shadow.'
What would you look like—like me? like your mother?
I possess one photo of Ida, a family snapshot,
she is posed with our father, her parents, her sister,
against the edge of a brick wall, some trees behind them.
She is lovely, of course, relaxed and contented;
he looks confident, handsome, they lean into each other.
I wish I could have met her. Absurd, I know,
but then I sometimes wish you could have met *my* mother—
is there a word for the bond that connects you?
Some things there are no words for. What were you feeling,
thinking, on that last walk you took together, to the left?
Did you cling tightly to your mother's hand?
Were you beside each other at the end, when the gas came?
What final desperate words did you exchange?
Some things there are no words for, unknowable.
Yet there are moments when I would like to know you.
Where are you now—in what unthinkable limbo?
Our father goes there, the past relives him in the dark,
he revisits that galaxy when he sleeps.
He has told me you were a beautiful child.
I try to picture you, though you never visit *my* dreams;
but I'm glad you're there, and proud that I carry your name.
If not for you, where would *I* be now?—I mean,
if not for the labyrinth, your innocent fate, your little life.
And so I speak to you like this—how else can I?
Until we meet in some unspeakable realm, look at each other
in that timeless, placeless domain, embrace and fall silent,
ghosts of the things we were, phantoms
of what might have been, and might have not.

— June 2012

The Dream

('El Sueño', Jorge Luis Borges)

If (as they say) a dream is like a truce,
no more than just a respite for the mind,
why, if you wake abruptly, do you find
you feel some thief has cut your fortune loose?
Why should the early morning be so sad?
It strips us of a gift that's inconceivable,
so intimate it is only retrievable
in trances that the vigil-hours have clad
with dreams whose golden glitter may betray
fragments from the treasure-store of darkness,
from a realm that is timeless and nameless,
distorted in the looking-glass of day.
Who will you be this evening, when you glide
over the dreamwall, to the other side?

Translated from the Spanish

Aubade, Allegro

'The past is never where you think you left it.'
— Katherine Anne Porter

A line of light from a passing van sweeps the ceiling
like a blade. Something becomes.
The days have tumbled—a snaking row of dominoes,
history in disarray. And then an intrusion
of thought as the zeros clatter their alarum.
You tap the phone, tapping blessed silence. Lately
the gender of trees, the dance of isobars, monuments
shifting and foolish ships colonize
your obsessions. In a sushi parlour you overheard
'Ah, yes, gravitas', and the rhyme wouldn't release you,
its satiric grin. Compulsive, you emailed it
to yourself, let it haunt the inbox unopened,
then a spark spoke up: Time is orthogonal, its walls sheer,
deceptive as glass, and the angles crawl
ever inwards and out, a *meandros* in four dimensions.
But the futility of this conceit washes over you,
sense collapses, and a police helicopter
is shredding the counterfeit quiet. You drift
downstairs—yesterday, where's yesterday? A line from
somewhere: May the end hold memory not misery …

You stop, listen. A piano's rhetoric has been looping
inside your skull: Sonata 18, that glorious leap
into bar 46—and gratitude lifts the hot urn, teaspoon
of brown dust, a quaver of milk. A bird, maybe
Beethoven himself, sweeps the window like a ghost.
You drum the keyboard bench, prepare to perform the day.

Trio with No Minuet

On this frosty mid-morning in August
    the philosopher tosses his tartan scarf
        back over his left shoulder like salt, steps

more briskly to pass a dejected apprentice
    attached vaguely to smoke who, dreading
        a fresh domestic, half-trips melodramatically,

turns theatrical to cast a quizzical dagger
    at the offending asphalt, surveyed by a girl
        fingering her metallic lip as if to reconfigure

old excuses for missing the train again,
    your train, the very one the philosopher
        swallows the rigid breeze to climb aboard,

rushing to oversee a seminar on why
    the examined life is not worth dying for,
        which you too had contemplated visiting

but have resolved instead to abide
    by the café window, regretting only
        the sheer impossibility of overhearing

what the sad apprentice has confided
    to the lip-girl, and why she has reached
        into her zebra handbag for a cracked phone

they are now jointly transfixed by,
    then grin into, then giggle, then disalign
        their heads and head off, slightly together.

Travellers

'In the rushing train only the future is real,
for every moment is given to a different place ...'
— Hermann Broch, *The Anarchist*

Just five of us in the carriage,
three with cords recharging their ears,
       and a fourth has periscoped
a palm-sized apparatus, and begins

to film the bleak suburban panorama
rolling past. As we're hushed
       into a tunnel he holds focus,
for his porthole is suddenly articulate

with mirages of the three women
sprinkled down the far side of the aisle.
       One of them has caught on,
darkens her regard, turns disdainful

to her own blackened window.
The traveller, chastened, dips his lens
       into a holster secreted below,
hoists a paperback with a German title

which, craning past his neck,
I disambiguate as *The Sleepwalkers*.
       Sensing espionage, he glares
at me through his dissolving mirror,

for the tunnel is being retracted,
the illuminated world invades the gloom
       and decelerates. I look about:
we have slotted ourselves into a station

and my traveller is chasing the corridor,
gaining on the girl who rebuked him.
       How much slighter she looks,
in her heels, clumping to the platform.

Profile

I watch him side-on. The left hand
gently palmed against his face,
elbow at rest beside the coffee cup,
right hand fisted to the other cheek.
He twists, twiddling his thoughts,
his spectacles flash like a shutter
under sunlight brittled from the street,
his tie is striped, diagonally,
in blue and white. Now he polishes
with fingertips the page he reads,
no, an iPad; his shoes are polished
too, he dredges with a spoon
the last of the latte bottoming his cup,
swivels, glances across. I pretend
total loss, put on that dreamy glaze
of the oblivious nonchalant, of one
deeply not there. He pushes back, chair
bellows at the wooden floor,
he rises, like a man where backpain
shadows every move, but the flap
of the lapel parts to reveal—
a revolver, slung from the shoulder
by a strap, staining the shirt and
darkening the day. This is not
the calling of the clerk I took him for.
He packs up his things, pivots
towards the door, straightens, sniffs,
dashes a tissue at his nostril, blows.
The flap re-shows, he pats down his side,
glances at me again, and—winks.
The kind of wink you get when you're
four or maybe five and a cloudy adult
who thinks you're cute then smiles
at your mother and says, *Nice little boy!*

—because the child-eyed stare
inspecting him has stirred perhaps
a joy at going home to his own
sweet son, or he fancies your mum,
or maybe he's just an amiable, innocent
passer-by, a man you'll never
see again, who never carries a gun.

Through the Window-Glass

Those wonderland people wanted her back,
   messages kept arriving;
But Alice had discovered an alternative track,
   in fact she was thriving.

On the tram each morning the town unfurled
   from her window-seat,
Where she read and reflected upon the world,
   her elbows discreet,

Watching the crowds rush around her, intent
   on looking and learning—
For she was staggered by this novel firmament,
   stung by a new yearning.

How could she scramble down that hole again,
   let alone even find it,
Now that she'd drunk of *this* wondrous domain,
   suddenly unblinded

And burning to investigate its pale population,
   their every hope and habit?
Only one thing gave her cause for speculation:
   everyone was a rabbit.

In Rehearsal

But there's always a but. First of all
the soundcheck bounced—so badly
that our fidgety MD managed to work
himself up into a major province
and all he got was vulgar feedback
from Katoomba (his tag for the tetchy
sibling trio of backing vocalistes) until
he thought he might as well fold back
into himself for the duration of a scotch,
since he was still sane enough to know
he was going mad. Then the strangest
amazement washed across his multifocals:
nothing he could see, of course; just
a kind of perhaps Dimple-induced calm
that had him quoting '*Everything matters*
and nothing matters' from somewhere
to himself, and once the euphoria
had percolated through him into a hazy
liquescent afterglow not utterly unlike
sex, he stood up, toppling a music-stand,
waved an arm ambiguously. 'Oh my
goodness gracious!' he cried. 'Take five,
take ninety-two, whatever. I just had this
awesome idea! Go home, guys—I'm going
to reorchestrate for air-guitar and strings!'

Sour Wine

'A glass apiece of red acrid *pinard*.'
     — e. e. cummings, *The Enormous Room*

There was an ode that wanted to be born
   somewhere within the pleasant bounds
     amid the corn
   and cornucopia and surrounds
not of a squalid garret, grim and torn,
of some ungainly rhymester gulping beer,
    but in a glorious way—
     that is to say,
within the garden of a wizard or vizir.

The birth was difficult. One would be wise
   neither to underestimate
     nor overprize
   the zeal we're prone to celebrate
as 'inspiration', when muse-dazzled eyes,
with the assurance of a practised hand,
    after a long dry spell
     think they foretell
genius at last restored. One needs to understand

the self-deceptions of a wishful mind,
   too ready to believe, to burn,
     and much too kind
   to its own creed, hot to discern
a gleaming diamond in an unrefined
nugget of carbon, its corners crumbling,
    its coloration drab—
     hardly the grab
at greatness from a vain versifier's fumbling.

Be that as it may be, one should concede
    that in this case all the stars looked
        aligned indeed
    for our poeticist, who brooked
no setback but by fronting it, for he'd
succeeded always deftly to resolve
        most problems with his prose
            as they arose,
and when it came to verse—he knew how to dissolve

whatever doubts a poem could produce.
    One day, however, he met up
        with an obtuse
    but otherwise quite pleasant pup
of a poetaster not hard to confuse
with the glib type I mentioned near the start,
        because in point of fact
            (suspending tact)
although in love with artistry, he lacked all art.

Suspecting this, the scribbler had imposed
    himself upon our poet's time:
        he had composed
    an ode without a decent rhyme
and scarcely any rhythm—and proposed
they should 'collaborate' on his attempt,
        and then submit the same
            in his own name,
for which a generous sum would make him exempt

(the cheat, I mean) from any later claim
    by the true author, such that his
        unholy fame
    would never be inferred amiss
by readers, and his counterfeited name

would grace the pages of anthologies
        on every bookish stand
            across the land:
a plan bereft of flaws—or of apologies.

One can report that our poetic friend
        (the proper one) was so enraged
            that in the end,
     having paced like a creature caged,
he decided: Yes!—he'd remould and mend
and *sharpen* this dull poem till it shone
        like a sword. Which he did.
           And then he slid
it into a yellow envelope as his own.

And all those books acknowledge me alone.

The Light We Convert

'There are only twelve notes. You must treat them carefully.'
(Paul Hindemith)

I *Prologue*

He complains his concentration grows worse.
—'Whatever I think, I'm thinking something else.'

He will not trust the night to comfort him.
—'When at last I fall asleep, it's only a dream.'

He purchases his misadventures on credit.
—'I'm frequently sorry, yet I seldom regret it.'

He wields his theology like a ringmaster's whip.
—'If a passage should rankle, I refigure it.'

He says it's the gods should be seeking asylum.
—'The gods are culpable, but who can blame them?'

He won't permit his epistemologies to show.
—'I do not know … If I knew, I'd know.'

II

Evenings are not to be trusted, each new morning
clears the mist exposed by retreating night.

Nor can you trust the night to comfort you—
whatever sleep encloses, day reopens it
with digital precision, rescored, remastered,

and all at once the music's playing faster,
redarkening the room. They say it's often said
that dreams reveal what we already knew;
that what we *think* we know, claiming the light,

lies to us. We sense miscomprehension dawning.
We blame the gods for leading us astray,
find solace in the stained-glass shards of day.

III

'My symphony is long and not exactly amiable.' (Brahms)

The crimson cleric, the congenial papa,
the marbled master, his temper never on edge,
the billiard-boy, and that fiery fist-shaker—

just several of the shades to whom I credit
my misadventures in Euterpe's realm.
I am a *fabbro* failed—
will my symphony ever see the light?

He dubs me apostle of music, while the gods
grin as I spar with the demon of my notes,
one eye on the future, the other fixated
on that stern jury. And to complicate life,
I'm hopelessly in love with my mentor's wife.

IV

There aren't too many things that I regret—
too little water under too few bridges,
the languages I'll never tell a joke in,
the times I knew I knew, yet acted else.

Not that I feel a need to apologize, mind you,
nor that the anecdotes I told seemed
inartistic, or that I harboured thinkings
dark or dangerous. No—just your random
lucky-dip of guilts I'd confess to confessing.

And in case you think I think you think I'm
a culprit, I remind you—only my art matters.
And art's a gift for which you don't apologize.

V

'I shall create a new world for myself.' (Chopin)

His precise contemporary from the east
has taken off and is living on that island
with his woman who is a man who is a woman;
how can he concentrate, with all those olive trees,
crusader churches, mosques—and then her?

Such a romantic! And yes, they call him poet
whenever he deigns to extemporize his skills;
but they say his other almost exact confrère,
that would-be Franciscan with vertiginous fingers,
is also her lover! Bully for him, I say;
but I wish I had a tenth of their dazzling talent
as I wrestle with this wretched oratorio.

VI

'Your epistemology's showing again …'
We tell her this deliberately to provoke her.
She preaches in our local Speakers' Alley,
trying to convince whoever's there, in vain,
how drink and dissolution choked her—
strangled her operatic voice. Well, her tally

she brags is impressive. Dozens converted
by her troubadour rhetoric, diverted
from 'meretricious haunts'—well, la-di-da!
(I must look up what epistemology means.)
We don't *know* what she knows—she seems
so much her own fantasy, with guitar.

VII

'I am a different kind of organism …' (Wagner)

The gossips ceremoniously proclaim
such love is sure to be the death of them—
illicit offspring of a magician, with that conjuror
of palaces in clouds, every stratagem
an insurrection to shake the concert-hall.
A generation younger, can she maintain
her mission as his muse, or must she fall

to a second loveless union? And he struts
about the city, puffed with ambition, sorcerer,
a brilliant bigot lunging for the flame
of immortality. Even N shuts his door to him
now. Yet music will never be the same.

VIII

Well, our Don at the very least was spared
the ravages of conscience in old age:
those three-and-thousand conquests he shared
with his capacious ego grew into a cage
for *les tous deux*, a prison *he'd* prepared,
and when the trapdoor opened, left-downstage,
and he peered into the chasm, and was falling,
he heard a voice he recognized too late, still calling.

We toil away, trusting our songs survive
their falser notes, and our own antiphonal state.
Not each of us can be a saintly scribe—
the passions from our pages must sing our fate.

IX

'… music which fills the soul with a thousand things
better than words.' (Mendelssohn)

Three centuries to the year, and to the year,
between you and red Harry, who quilled as well
(they say) his clutch of wordless songs,
collecting instruments and wives along the way.
While, on this side of time, you pipped
your close contemporaries by a page of months,
and your most acrid critic by near forty-eight.
You and your too-shadowed sibling,
three summers older, made a splendid comet

with a double tail. Racing the harder, she burned free
first—robbing you both, and us, of the irony
of a *Ring* you planned that now would never be.

X

With cathedral reverence I try to control
what I am thinking as I watch her play.
No, only the music, I command myself—
and I close my eyes to no longer see her.
Is she oblivious, can she be unknowing
of my distractedness? This trite bagatelle
slipping her fingers just sweetens my torment.
Is there a physick that could calm this fever?
I struggle to listen, she finishes, closes
the keyboard and turns and then pauses.

And says: 'Focus on those scales until they flow.
Your wrists will loosen, your control will grow.'

XI

*'Only when the form grows clear to you, will the spirit
become so too.'* (Schumann)

So what of mornings—can they be better trusted
than evening or night? Can we be sure
what the new day exposes with kindly clarity
is not simply a manner of retreating
from what we know, deep in a subterranean
cavern, deeper than any nightmare, any dream?
Are all our fears and fabrications what they seem?
And what propels that vulnerable or vain
compulsion to create, construct, compose our fleeting
tilt at cathedrals, sunken or becalmed; the alacrity
of our stubborn will to build what we think is true?
I do not know—only that time is brief, and we must trust it.

XII *Coda*

Just as these lines have led a path less clear
than camouflaged, where rhyme and reason play
their guessing-game, where hints and twists appear,

a sixfold catechism having paved the way;
so the regrets we claim, the light that we convert
to knowledge, the dark to ambiguous day,

combine (if we are so inclined) to reassert
themselves in the song we compose. I chose a brace
of years from a slice of time, strove to insert

some threads conjoining them. But any place
and any art would do, and any year.
Are not the dreams we fashion, the dreams we chase?

The Other Side

Audi partem alteram (St Augustine)

If I could be certain about *my* city
I would not be proposing this;
see, there are too many documents,
they sail across our unshuttered window
each eventide and vanish
somewhere right-angled to the sky.
You lied (no?)
when you accused the sky of hypocrisy—
it means everything it says, just
doesn't twig too deftly
to the inherent duplicities of the cosmos:
strong force, weak force, strings
open and closed, what a recital!
A garret above she's reciting Mandelbrot
into her cups, alert poet
not yet alarmed, the appointment
a week away. Will there be fire? Or is it
great Anaximander I mishear
at the harpsichord, desperate to reconcile
his celestial wheel with equal temperament?
Meanwhile stationary old Earth
heaves a soiled sigh of hope, we wait
in trepidation for the timid boy next door
to start repounding his weights
or curl his bicep to lubricious pixels
that constellate the black hole of his lair.
I conjure all those nuclear *familiae*
with their duple single beds,
the Crux of the South cartwheeling
over the rotary hoist, every last parchment
secure in its slot, each element tipsy
with itself, still writhing under the table.
Where are you, Democritus,
and what about all those atoms?

The Glovebox Dispensary

Up at the Old Jefferson they're chuckling
over their cabernets, arguing over small beers—
the dental nurse whose boss will caress her
cheek for another month; the weepy genarian,
octo, nona, who has just discovered a cure
for cancer, his latest amazing MRI; the cabman
with the falling flag, alert for a hail, a glovebox
his dispensary ('the big V: never lets me down!');
the professor's protégée with her Sexton thesis
first-classed already by the poet she loves, alive
only in his departmental clasp. That's just
a taster—there's the CEO, Estelle, whose partner
roams the galleries scouting for fresher art,
he knew Whiteley (personally: they were like
this!) back in the sixties; and old McHale, he took
Mr Eternity's hand when Stacey (he calls him)
went astray one day casing the Cross; nobody
really believes them, or little Max who claims
he jammed with Satchmo, Cleveland, '48.
But this is Friday night, the claymen's *kiddush*,
all the cloned girls' benediction. Candlelight
and tipsy brazen their coin, singe their perukes,
commerce ricochets round the temple pediments;
the Doric columns lean in, listening for clues.

Barcarolle

The piano-player holding the café corner
    seldom looks up from his instrument, afloat
on his own private current, devoid of history,
    vacant of thought. The archway
behind the piano, behind him, is leaning back
    against its arch nature, distorted
as in a funfair mirror; the gilded chandelier
    due north is straining in its sockets, would
descend, would droop, magneted by music,
    another waltz by Lugubrianov,
a further Fauré barcarolle, a morose ballade;
    three scattered patrons oversit their coffees,
their toast with confiture, without noting
    anything aesthetic; they had exchanged
cursory nods on entering, on easing down to order,
    that's it, just an open *Times* or *Figaro*
commands each lethargic view; the grizzled waiter
    practises the air of a dilettante at rest,
conjectures his next event, his certain customer
    who will stride inside, settle a spot
diagonally distant from the recital-stand, unfold
    a book fat with Cyrillic secrets,
tamp down the pages and doze off to await his bun
    and brew. The player at the pianola
in the corner looks up for the first time, searches
    once more for that brown-haired girl
from the other day, her flimsy sandwich, her teacup:
    all he wants to do is meet her eye.

Apokryphon

Midnight dream. The bed swims beneath a roof awash
with the rid remains of hags and queasy clocks.

On the stead a pair of hungover jocks. The guests gather
all over again. The wedding canopy's lid

is quilted with cartoons in black pen, pastels, and prints
of exotic family trees. Invitees lavishly grin, some of them weep.

A leering urchin passes, waltzing with a broom. Curtains
part, discreet. Soon the speeches will start, the blackening sky

and canopy refill, umbrellas are crisply arranged.
The marriage of pride and gloom. All manner of vows shall be

exchanged, while the uninvited clutter about in a forbidden room.
No tickets please. On the lawn, a slightly familiar singing

among contorted trees, a plinkle of glasses and a tlunk of plates.
Eyes crawl everywhere, looking for links. Sex and seduction

colonize the air, it's a cocktail turn: he's itching for some
fingerfood, she scans for drinks. Wait, is that the celebrant

pushing the gates, wearing her tinny sprinkle of professional joy?
Her golden tresses, the way she flings them, gorgeously. Oh boy!

(Among the rhododendrons, behind the drive, a churl wrestles
with a virgin's brief, watches her arrive. Maybe now

the reception can begin.) But the celebrant isn't: she's merely
another guest; rumours fly. The sated couple from the bushes

remingle at the rotunda, offer each other the rosy eye.
On the balcony a tipsy-curvy secretary strips. The midnight dreamer,

disabused, notes how it really is clothes that naketh the woman.
She vanishes behind a vase. Everybody sips.

War Disposal

He wears black—gunslinger black.
Can be readily distracted but quick to draw
hazy conclusions from hinted asides.
A grudge he will never bear, though he burns
incense to appease the merest slight
misunderstanding with sweet smoke. Smoking
he repudiated decades back, but will chew
cheap leaves he claims he bought online
from Cuba. The Bermuda Triangle obsesses
some of the vets he meets at Valentino's
but he, indifferent to the Caribbean, chooses
to navigate aboard a book channelling
the Prince, or Poitiers, or some sundry Pope,
while at night scribbling poems derived
scrutably from Zane Grey's essays on man.
He *would* have served in the Forces
if his eyesight had let him, the sergeant
recruiting laughed out loud when he misread
an E for a Z on the top row, stopped him
right there and shook his pencil. Yet
he can pore over illuminated uncials until
kingdom come, preferably Plantagenet
because he always did adore the eroticism
of the Lancasters, has flown many nightmares
as a tail-arse Charlie, and the RAF for him
would have been a no-brainer but that sarge
was unbribable. So he wears black—
garnished with sunglass goggles from a war
disposal store up in Lower George Street,
near the Chinese restaurant he'd once taken
his one-and-only lady companion to, his
sole-and-single one-night stand that morphed
into an aircrash and him into a lonesome
cowboy, retired would-be gunner, armchair
troubadour, deposed dauphin, whatever.

The Puddle

Is it a sleep-line or the script of age?
Cross-examining glass, she thumbs the crease
    until it glows, bends to the bed again
and tiptoes into her slippers, fusty
from too much floor. Her cellphone drums

on the dresser, she swipes it clean,
trapezing over the bedspread to retrieve
    the jeans draped like a waterfall
to dry indoors from last evening's storm,
their failed conciliation, the sour words

she texted an hour later. The venetian spills
its slanted avalanche into the difficult
    penumbra of her mood, accelerates
her mechanized dressage about the room,
before she hurtles down the Persian stairs

into the kitchen, where cigarettes
and aftershave still overtone his lurid
    accusations, his sanitized denials,
circling her with doubt—until she lights
upon the hollowed cabernet, a chair askew

where he had jettisoned his rhetoric
like a loser sweeping the chessboard clean,
    to thump the passage, stomp out with a slam.
She strides past the grim umbrella-stand,
its puddle gone; takes aim, and boots the door.

Diminished Light

The little girl in the laundromat
is sitting so still
she could be a mirage. What
is she thinking, watching a sky crawl
with purple? Soon its shell
will crack, and rolled umbrellas
under everyone's arm will billow

into their mushroom dance,
and her mother watching the porthole
where a world spins will take
her by the arm, and soon she'll fall
into her usual
late-afternoon haze as they cross
the glistened street, no less

and no more distant than before,
the wind clouding her face
the way the shopfronts suddenly share
diminished light, the way no voice
could say her sadness,
make real the little girl
hopping alongside, hungry bird.

Stubborn Streak

Rummaging in the dark web of his attic,
he resurrects a secret envelope flush
with erotic drawings—his adolescent artistry
of discovery and want. In a Brillo carton,
the red firetruck, its extension-ladder thread
still intact; a Coca-Cola yoyo; the silver
magician's-box with its cram of vivid silks
crumpled within; a low-rise keep of college
lecture-notes under the dormer window;
and on a shelf of the tall secretary-desk,
graduation token from his parents, a stack
of albums. He lifts the topmost, blows away
the dust, opens at random. Monochrome

snapshot—the two stand close together
by the water's edge, terrytowel swimshorts,
a trim bikini, his arm claims her, they smile.
Twenty-two, they'd met at a youth convention
in Miami, hit it off. He liked her well enough,
he liked her shape, she was smart and sweet,
and sentimental. Within a month she'd migrated
all the way to Boston to be near him, preceded
by a guarded call from her Denver dad
to suss him out, and to warn that his daughter
had a stubborn streak. Nothing came of it,
he couldn't find the heart to commit, learnt later
that she'd stayed and married, a jeweller from
Montevideo. Probing a drawer, he digs out

a wad of letters, its rubber-band in bits
tracking the bundle with their brittle Morse.
His first love—callow, captivating,
studiously unconsummated. Both nineteen,

they'd weathered stern parental disapproval
in the Verona of '60s New England. A year
it lasted, he couldn't find the heart to commit,
till she wrote to tell him she'd met someone,
an older man, a teacher from Grand Junction,
really sorry. She hoped he would one day
find what he was seeking, signed off
with a row of exes trailing into the margin.
He refolds the letter, scrapes at the dead
elastic, shuts the drawer. His iPhone pings:
he's late for that wretched anniversary.

Cryptic Crosswords

'Same again!' he called from his corner
   by the window to the sad brunette behind the bar.
She confirmed, so he rejoined the cryptic
   he'd begun on the train from Montreal, the world
outside a blank of all-devouring white.
   By Schenectady he'd given up, decided to leave
the puzzle half-cracked till he got to Penn.
   New York was bleak, an icy January wind scoured
the taxi-ranks as he dragged his suitcase
   toward the next yellow blob steaming at the curb,
headlights drizzling. The cabbie, shadowy
   and sullen, grumbled at the three-dollar gratuity
he'd pressed into his glove at journey's end,
   the Roosevelt on Madison and East 45th. Adding
a five, he trusted his bag to a bouncy porter
   prowling the sidewalk. Sharp rain slanted straight
into his cheeks, he felt a spasm of unease—
   especially once he spotted his wife in the lobby,
pointing irritably into her Tissot, spoiling
   for argument. He performed an eye-rolling shrug
up into the ostentatiously faceted ceiling.
   She stood up to welcome him, they embraced like
hypocrites. Surely the divorce documents
   had come through? He could hardly wait to settle
everything, get back to his favourite bar
   on 51st, his cryptics, downing alternate espressos
and Edradours, rare specialty of the house.
   They'd agreed to meet in the morning for the ride
to the attorneys'. But now, casing his suite,
   he recalled the white train, brightened, stripped
to his t-shirt in the oppressive central heat,
   unfolded the damp *Times*. That pesky 49-across.

Incipit

When the words refused to dance
he would sweep his palm like some lout
across the Olivetti's keys, causing
the letters on their metal stalks to bristle
a Mexican wave in the machine's
half-moon amphitheatre. Fresh flesh:
he needed sinewy heat. His lines dragged

their tails along, skin-and-bones prose
clad in glitz-cool paraphernalia
yet skeletal for all that. Trial by error—
he suspected he'd abandoned himself
somewhere behind the last semi-passable
rendezvous with art. Nowadays
he'd ball up each new stillborn incipit,

grab the Greek cap that dangled
like a taunting modifier from the knob,
sling a checkered scarf round his collar
and head for a fix to Jink's, a favoured bar
on 18th Street where he was assured
of faintly sympathetic raillery from Eevee
(yes, she spelt it thus). One day

he'd have her, he declaimed. And one day,
more than notably drunk, he'd risked
kissing her stubborn lips while stuffing
a C-note down her t-shirt (*Keep the change!*).
Yet nothing ever helped. If just,
he lashed himself, those rich imaginings
could migrate onto the empty page.

But the words refused to dance
to any song but none—no song, they danced
the same no-song as she. So he ditched
the Olivetti, wangled a one-way ticket
to Mediterranean shores. The Levantine air
might bring aesthetic repair. And hey—
plenty more palindromes in *that* sea.

Rooftops

Jeffrey Smart (1968–69)
Joseph Brown Collection, NGV, Melbourne

for Philip Salom

He is lying sprawled within one of the spaces
        between the spaces,
dreaming of a perfect seven-eyed pavilion
        in burnt sienna, at rest
behind bars under a gun-grey broth drinking
        the Rome air naked.

In his dream he computes a pert little flowerpot
        in the one unblinded window
at his back, and he conjures an enchanted cable
        slung across the chasm
from his *terrazzo* to those blushing geraniums,
        which he will pluck
and offer to *her*, the lovely *principessa* of the Dish,
        imprisoned for epochs
behind a bravado of bricked-up oval apertures
        and cruelly lorded over
by this lurid deconstructed meccano mushroom,
        terrible, toxic and grotesque.

But how will he then clear the second precipice
        (given a safe return to balcony)
to broach her? Another tightrope? In his reverie
        he scans the skyline's horizon—
perhaps that corner ledge like a leftover stub
        is a clue, a sign, a foothold;
yet even if he managed to overleap that limbo
        and grasp the cornerstone

and writhe up onto the deck—will she still
        want him? And what if
he slipped, plummeting headlong into the waiting
        unknown abysses below?

Or—what if he's captured by the gloating molester
        and strapped for all time
to that rusty scaffold, or nestled and riveted,
        a modern Prometheus,
into its curvature, to rotate like a rock staring forever
        into naked dreamless space?

After Jacqmin

Is not the snowy plain
as tricky as a well-turned phrase?
— The Book of the Snow

Snow understands the necessity for discretion,
knows which rock to cover
which doorstep to conceal.
When it sighs from the sky it is soundless,
like memory's white pulse;
yet among the alps of imagination
remembrance can dislodge an avalanche,
while the lowlands blanketed in guilty slumber
tremble against the blissful
drizzle of forgetting.

Prognosis

(1185 BCE)

I slip inside each afternoon to observe the progress
of construction. This immense creature,
its woven timbers planed, adorned and lacquered,
will be thirty cubits tall, or so they tell me.
I marvel at such hubris, secretly. Can they believe
      that the gates will be flung wide to welcome it,
      that it will not be unmasked for the treachery it is,
      that its cavernous bowels will not smother
the forty doomed heroes destined to ride within?
I can foresee the Phrygians, straight alert to the ruse,
admitting the beast, towing it onto the marketplace—
then setting their torches to it! Can glimpse already
the horrified occupants, aflame, screaming,
tumbling from its hold, all their spears and machines
useless against a firestorm whose savage fury
will amaze even mighty Olympus.
                       O Troy,
I fear that we labour in vain to vanquish you,
      that your city will yet abide a thousand years,
      that a thousand wars will not win your demise,
      that the gods will ensure your fame is celebrated
long after untold towns on the Great Sea's edge are dust.

The Achaeans understand nothing of History;
they laugh, carouse, their Horse grows daily more arrogant.
Some nights I weep for the fate that I know attends them.

Stylite

St Simeon of Aleppo (AD 453)

My obelisk is my home,
I need no other.

For thirty years now I have lived
Atop this pillar,
Six square yards crowded
With my devotion.

You come to gaze
Up at me from the footing
Fifty feet below,
Wonder at the limits
Of my endurance, ask
Each other how I can attend
To daily necessities:
There are other necessities,
My friends, and there are ways.

Far harsher when the winds
Lash my supplications or the rains
Drench my sacred bond or
The desert's tongue scorches
My worthless flesh:
But longing for the foul earth
Below has never flagged
My spirit all these
Seasons, their eleven
Hundred nights
That pass in exultant prayer.

Nor will I descend
Before I touch the clouds at last
With completed eyes.

Passarola

Bartolomeu de Gusmão (1685–1724)

I

I was no Icarus, yet I flew too high.
It was a week before Christmas that I was born,
gazing to Heaven, or so the legend went—
but it wasn't because I was hearing the call of God,
or of Science; nor, as one scribbler insisted,
did I emerge awestruck to be sharing my birth
with those three melodious souls across the Atlantic.
No, not music was to be my calling: I would quest
after an earthlier loftiness. And I would dream.
Francisco and Maria, devoted parents, sent me
at fifteen to the Jesuits at Bahia; but no seminary,
no Society could contain me. I sailed for Lisbon,
blossomed at Coimbra: I read Mathematics,
Physics, Philology, I learnt languages, mastered
the Art of Memory. And I thought. Already,
my callow studies in Brazil had hatched a device
whereby water could be lifted uphill from a stream—
my earliest success with levitation.

II

My chance epiphany was a soap-bubble
I watched floating up in the hot glow of a candle.
An object could be made to rise through heat alone!
I thought about this. King João listened when I claimed
I could make an apparatus *walk on air*. My first try,
a balloon of paper, burnt before it could fly; next,
a similar contrivance rose 20 *palmos* before servants
destroyed it lest the palace ceiling be engulfed.
But third time lucky: on the eighth day of August,

in the year of our Lord, 1709, before the King,
his Queen, Cardinal Conti (our future Pope Innocent)
and an astonished court on the patio of the Casa da Índia,
my bird *rose*—until the flame failed, and she dropped
into the Palace Square. The first flying machine
lighter than air! Our King was hugely impressed,
heaped honours upon me, granted me the sole right
to build airships, with death to any who dared
to copy my ideas. Even I thought that last a bit harsh.

III

By combustion, my balloon had raised aloft
a metal ball in a basket. It was a start. I continued
to refine my *Passarola* while drafting other designs.
I envisaged a vessel with wings, bellows, a tail,
wind-tubes and inflated globes. I conceived a craft
built around a pyramid of gas. So much to think of!
But stretching for clouds, I had grown too visible—
my inventions reached the nose of the Inquisition.
I was deemed a heretic; others called me wizard!
Burning my papers, I fled in disguise to Spain,
hoping for England. It was not to be.
Brought low by pernicious fever, I succumbed
at Toledo, unready and, alas, too young—
yet consoled by the splendour of my achievement.
After all, had I not conquered the miracle
of flight, three generations before those two
upstart French balloonists?—and who can reckon
how many centuries since ill-starred Icarus!

Antietam

'Truth is known only to its victims.
All else is photographs …'
    — Douglas Dunn, 'I Am a Cameraman'

I was drifting in silence through a labyrinth
labelled *Images of the Civil War*,
trying to picture myself in Mathew Brady's place,
or that of the utopian Alexander Gardner,
how each must have recoiled from those scenes
where his lens registered, faithful,
merciless, the faces and the bodies of men
frozen forever at that zero moment
when their quotidian journeying must collide
with the ageless contortions of the planets—
when, like Vesuvian ash, the eruption
of light would immortal their monochrome fate
onto an innocent membrane of glass,
their ghosts imprisoned to stare from the panels
that now alone etched their singular trace.
                                        I paused
at the display charting the bloodiest encounter
(23,000 dead or wounded in a single day),
my eye drawn to a fallen Rebel, his hand
half-raised in futile supplication, his gaze
probing past mine with such urgent knowledge
that I turned away to see what lay behind.
But all I could fix upon was a child
pointing toward some spot I could not discern,
sobbing inconsolably, tugging at her father;
and I was consoled enough to return
to the Passion on the wall, confounded enough
to evade my Confederate's accusing stare.

Sixteen Men

Clouds roll over the swift forest
like time-lapse photography. They break
in waves across the sky, a few droplets
float on the wind. The sixteen men

stand on the edge of the ditch they have dug
with their own hands. No longer can they see
the clouds, their eyes have been shielded
from the glare of their fate. No longer

can they turn to each other, as they did
in the open truck that has brought them here.
No longer can they sing their songs of hope
and freedom as they did at night, softly

in darkened barracks. The sixteen men
stand, their faces to the pit they have hollowed
with their own hands, then—drop
to their knees as if in prayer and topple

forward into the grave they have prepared
with their own hands. Their forms rustle
as they slide into freshened earth.
Four other men come forward to inspect

the task they have achieved. They move
rapidly, blanketing their work with shovels,
grunting from the strain of earth against metal.
Silent, they climb aboard the truck

idling close by, two in the cabin,
two in the empty tray. The youngest
picks up a shoe from the slatted floor,
hurls it onto the unsettled soil. Tomorrow

they will return in the same truck, no longer
as four other men, but crowded together
and shivering with a dozen others.
Four of the next sixteen.

Skull

The memory circles but never lands,
precarious as that cloudless night in spring
during a long, unspecified campaign
that none of us understood.
We'd heard about Thermopylae, Masada,
our chronicles lit up the Punic Wars,
we knew the lore of blood about Gallipoli
and the Levant. Nothing like this—
here we seemed supremely unaware of
where we were, where we were
going to go, what we were meant to do.
No maps, no charts, no battle plan;
simply they'd dropped us on this cursèd
mountaintop, this skull high up above a city
whose name nobody knew, not even
our taciturn commanders, and not a hint
of the race or faith of the inhabitants—
whose soundless airships almost every day
would drone some species of surveillance
over our sanctuary, such as it was, yet
never deigned descending to an altitude
to gun or greet us, or identify themselves,
expose their language, litter us with words
or pictograms, if that was what it took
to make connection with our mute intent—
which must have puzzled, or maybe amused,
a people (was it such?) whose vehicles,
down there below, far as the eye could reach,
moved with no lucid purpose or design …

Thus had the winter lapsed, without event.
But on that night, when the moon was down,
they ventured, at last, to assail our citadel—
not by a mode of weaponry we could name

but by this ghostly *whisper* rising from below,
growing loud, louder, and then erupting
into a chorus that transfixed me like a spear.
Its memory still circles, claws at my dreams
ready to pierce; yet it never lands. I only know:
the carnage we unleashed that night, the city
we annihilated in our grand, despairing,
barbarous reply, will tarnish for all time
these shiny coins that camouflage my chest.

Unspoken Sky

(*after Tina Makereti*)

It arrived unannounced, looked around
and sank into a slumber. The street-animals
walked by, oblivious. The machines wheeled
as they must. The towers leaned into themselves
whenever it turned its face to the sky.
The sky itself said nothing, in the way of skies,
but streamed with a forgiving light.

It awoke, forgiven, unaware it had been gazing
upward, squinting with eyes closed against
the unspoken sky. It stood, looked around,
and began to walk. The street-animals
stopped to watch, the machines pulled up,
grimly attentive. The towers frowned
and their perspectives corrected themselves.

At last the sky opened its eye and the eye
laughed, in the manner of the blind,
the seeing unseeing blind. It walked on,
disturbed by something approaching thought,
but clearer than any words, sadder
than any sigh, deeper than the oceans
that had given it birth. There was no going back.

Non-Incident at the Vienna Opera

(8 May 1906)

'History, like the universe which it is said to represent,
has a real and an ideal aspect.' (Goethe)

It refuses to release me, that encounter
    among the standing-only at the Wiener Hofoper.
It was the third act of *Tristan*, a restlessness

    had descended upon me—the pallid stagelight
perhaps, or a sudden impatience:
    a reflection of the mystic atmosphere.

He stood next to me, gazing fixedly into space,
    visibly transported by the drama,
a shortish nondescript youth scarcely sixteen.

    As I observed him, not furtively enough,
he met my eye, and (how can I explain?) a revulsion,
    no, a *terror*, such as I'd never known

overtook me. I had come to see Mahler conduct,
    but the spell of the music was broken
and I caught myself rehearse a shocking impulse:

    to reach into my coat for my penknife
and to *plunge* it into the neck of this total stranger!
    He was clapping furiously

as the opera ended, his torso and (to me) despicable
    expression perfectly rigid now
as if detached from the hands that, like his eyes,

appalled me more than I could fathom;
and had I but drawn that knife, plaything though it was,
   which with every rational sinew I resisted,

I believe I *would* have stabbed him, over and over,
   until that limp and dreaded form
twitched all but lifeless on the bloodied floor

   while I awaited the police in tranquil relief.
But all at once the vileness of my murderous fantasy,
   the humiliation of its execrable intent,

swept through me—I wrenched hold of my emotions
   and, desperate now to manufacture
some outer amends for an inner frenzy so unlike me,

   I sought his eye again. Willing myself to hold his gaze
I smiled pathetically, uttered some inanity
   to mollify my blazing conscience, reassure myself

(and him) in case he had detected the merest inkling
   of my demeanour. If a bit distracted,
he was jovial enough, we even exchanged names!

   I felt unburdened at first—yet the memory
continued to haunt me: not once in my twenty-odd years
   had I suffered such a moment's

abdication of reason, so destructive a passion;
   not even during this moronic war, where I squat,
a decade later, in an infernal trench

   on what last summer was a gentle Belgian meadow,
to compose this. Because that night,
   as the crowds dispersed and the hall lit up again

and I could finally evaluate his features clearly,
    my shame redoubled—he looked
merely alone and down-at-heart, though his eyes

    still glowed with embers of the music
that had so marvelled him. Going our separate ways
    we saluted each other like acquaintances.

Oddly enough I can't recall his name—Alfons
    or Aldo, something of the sort;
but my cheek burns when that evening swims before me

    or assails me in a dream, and I tremble even now,
on this accursed battlefield, to think
    of what I, an ordinary man, was almost capable.

For Length of Days

Canzone

What song is this? I want to rescue you,
from *diese Töne*—tones you should disown
yet can't discard. I watch and wait, while you
sustain your agitated air. With you
that song repeats itself, time after time;
it is as though its discord straddles you
and nothing can release, unravel you—
nothing to modulate or to replace
your stubborn rootlessness, a sense of place
plotted to no home key. I reckon you
kept emptying yourself of fullness till
you forfeited the art of standing still.

The decades multiply our flags and still
we dwindle further with each anthem. You
presume to navigate this ocean, still
locate a landfall, find that soft and still
centre the poets eulogize, your own
perfect oasis—yet the storm will still
rage all around you, and the world will still
smash each illusion you attach to time,
every mirage, until there comes a time
when no melodious fancy can instill
meaning into your music; when to place
your faith in faith usurps your truer place.

So what am I to tell you? How to place
in crystal sharpness everything you still
misapprehend?—that there is no such place
as paradise (I know you know)? No place

and no belief can fill the void that you
contend against; because if such a place
existed, or could be conceived in place
of this frail planet that we call our own,
you would renounce it!—because then your own
pitiful, sweet remembrance of *this* place
(for worse or better), *this* overdressed time,
would strip you naked, one strand at a time.

History has no patience, and no time
or sympathy for those who long to place
their mystic badge upon some bygone time
when 'light' prevailed. There was no such time
—brash history disabuses us—and still,
all the old shibboleths resurface, time
and again, seductive, until with time
we start to embrace them—not unlike you,
for all your learnèd rhetorics. Yes, you,
haunted by a Hell that suspended time,
you above all should make this truth your own:
what we cannot discard, we're doomed to own.

I am no Virgil—it is on your own
that you must make your reckoning with time.
You'll need raw nerve, the vision to be shown
every delusion that impedes your own
emancipation—never let's misplace
the dazzling, daring legacy we own,
an earth that we have scratched and soiled and sown,
and travelled end to end, and travel still,
not always certain where to go, but still
claiming each destination as our own.
No other journey can I offer you,
no other joy. Your rescue's up to you.

Well, I have had my say. Now only you
can summon up the passion that might still
transpose this time-worn, enigmatic place
into a key that could reconquer time.
A world truly our equal, and our own.

Inferno, Canto I

(from *The Divine Comedy* by Dante Alighieri)

Midway along the journey we call our life
    I found myself within a dark forest,
        having strayed from the path that was straight.

Ah, how difficult it is now to record it,
    that savage wood, rugged and wild—indeed
        the very thought brings back the terror of it:

so bitter was it, barely less so than death!
    But to impart something of the good I gained,
        I'll tell of the other things I discovered there.

I can't with any certainty explain
    how I came into it: a sleepiness had seized me
        just at the point where I lost the rightful way.

But when I reached the bottom of a hill—
    where that valley could extend no further
        which had transfixed my heart with so much fear—

I lifted up my eyes and saw its shoulder
    already dressed in the warm rays of the planet
        that guides us on the straight road everywhere.

At this, I found that the fear which had persisted
    within my heart's lagoon during that night
        I had so bleakly spent, was somewhat allayed.

And just as one who, gasping to survive,
    escapes the sea and clambers to the shore
        then back to the deadly water turns his eye,

so my own mind, still running on and on,
    turned to take in again that pass from which
        no one had ever come out alive before.

Once I'd refreshed my weary limbs a while
        I pushed ahead along the deserted slope,
        the firmer foot always the one downhill.

And there, quite near to where the hillside rose,
        a leopard stood, nimble and very sleek,
        whose form was covered in a coat of spots.

Confronting me, it shadowed each step I took;
        so boldly did it hinder my ascent
        that more than once I thought of turning back.

The hour was early, morning had begun;
        the sun was climbing with those several stars
        which had accompanied him when Love Divine

first set in motion all good things that are;
        so that the time of day, and the sweet season,
        gave me good cause for hopefulness to brave

that curious animal with the festive skin.
        But not enough! for a new dread assailed me:
        just up ahead, there now appeared a lion.

It seemed that he was coming at me directly,
        head held high, the hunger so ferocious
        the very air seemed to be set trembling;

and then—a she-wolf, her wasted frame famished
        and full of craving, well enough renowned
        for causing many folk to live in anguish.

Her sight so terrified me, and a burden
        of such heaviness descended on my heart,
        that I gave up the hope of climbing on.

And just as one who, steeped in his many gains,
        one day discovering that all is lost,
        can only think to weep and bewail his fate,

so was I vexed by that relentless beast
    which, still advancing on me, inch by inch
    made me retreat out of the sun's caress.

As I dropped back, down to a lower place,
    before my gaze a form materialized,
    of one who seemed feeble from long silence.

On seeing him within that wilderness,
    'Have pity on me,' I cried, 'whatever you are:
    whether a living man or mere ghost.'

He answered: 'I *was* a man once, but no longer;
    my parents were of solid Lombard stock,
    and both of them were citizens of Mantua.

Though rather late, I was *sub Julio* born,
    and lived in Rome under the good Augustus
    during the time of false, deceitful gods.

A poet was I, and often sang the praise
    of Anchises' noble son who came from Troy
    after proud Ilium was consumed in flames.

But why do *you* return to such dismay?
    Why aren't you climbing the delightful mount,
    the beginning and the source of all joy?'

'Are you, then, Virgil, that very fountain
    from which there flows so grand a river of words?'
    I answered him, feeling my forehead redden.

'O honoured, glorious light among the poets!
    May it now serve me, the long and loving labour
    that drew me on to dwell within your works.

You are my master, and indeed my author,
    it is from you alone that I derived
    the worthy style that has won me honour.

See that beast there, from which I turned aside:
      rescue me from her, my illustrious sage—
      she makes my pulse tremble, and my blood rise.'

'What you must do is take another path,'
      he answered when he saw that I was weeping,
      'if you want to escape this savage place;

because that beast, the cause of what you're feeling,
      permits no person ever to pass through,
      but whom she thus detains, she ends up killing;

for she, by nature, is malevolent and cruel,
      her raging appetite is never sated,
      and having fed, she hungers for yet more food.

Many the creatures are with whom she's mated,
      and many will be—until the Greyhound comes,
      to expedite her death in doleful pain.

He will not feed on territory or plunder,
      only on wisdom, love and decency;
      his land will lie between Feltro and Feltro.

Saviour he'll be of that poor Italy
      for whom virgin Camilla, Euryalus, Turnus
      and Nisus once were wounded mortally.

Through every city he will give her chase
      until he's put her back in Hell again,
      where Envy first accomplished her release.

My thought is, therefore, that your safest plan
      is to follow me: I will be your guide—
      and lead you hence through an eternal realm,

where you will hear endless despairing cries,
      see ancient spirits sunk in such distress
      that each screams out to die a second time;

and then you'll see those happy to persist
within the fire, because they hope to join,
when the time comes, the circles of the blessed:

though if you would ascend to that domain,
another soul will take you, worthier than I;
I will depart, while you with her remain.

You see, the Emperor who rules those heights,
because I was rebellious to his writ,
will not allow me entrance to his city;

boundless his dominion, he reigns absolute—
there is his city, his tall throne of state:
O happy those he chooses to admit!'

And I to him: 'Poet, I beg you by the grace
of that same god you do not claim to know,
help me to flee this wickedness, and worse;

lead me to where you spoke about before,
that I might come to see St Peter's gate,
and those you have described who suffer so.'

Then he moved off; I followed in his wake.

Translated from the Italian

Letters from the Periphery

'The work of the philosopher consists in assembling reminders for a particular purpose.'

— Ludwig Wittgenstein

[i]

We have never met, you do not know me,
So forgive me for being this forward,
But I needed to make contact, for reasons
That I hope will soon become evident.
I ask only that you do not read this message
(And others I may send from time to time)
In a spirit of misunderstanding or anxiety,
Or a sense that I am someone to be feared.
Nothing could be further from the truth.

[ii]

I do not really expect you to respond,
Or not just yet, so I trust that you will let me
Offer you these notes intermittently.
And do not think, please do not imagine,
That I harbour some deep ulterior motive
Which will play itself out at your expense.
Because much as I would like to meet you,
I do not wish to violate your privacy
Or approach you without your permission.
But I shall continue to watch over you
(Think of me as a kind of guardian spirit):
I will be satisfied to gaze from the periphery,
Content to admire you from afar.

[iii]

I wonder if you have read the philosophers.
There is a river and there is Heraclitus
And he tells us it is never the same river,
That it changes from moment to moment
Because change is the essence of the world.
I passed you seven days ago
As you hurried across St Cecilia Square
(White t-shirt, blue jeans, brown satchel):
Our eyes touched—the flimsiest of moments.
But within that moment I was plunged
In the river of you, of our destiny—
A river that flows through me as I write,
A river that (forget Heraclitus)
Is changeless, and eternal, and divine!
For I knew there and then—you were mine.

[iv]

I am sorry if that sounded melodramatic
(I hope my zeal did not alarm you),
But one should never bridle zealousness.
I have explored the great minds of the ages,
The poets, philosophers, historians,
And concluded that the *second* golden rule
(No lesser than the one more renowned)
Is to speak at all times with sincerity—
To be honest, with oneself and others,
And without embarrassment or hesitation
Acknowledge and declare one's true feelings.
It is in that spirit of openness
(Which I trust will cause you no discomfort)
That I post these fond communications.

[v]

I came across this in Schopenhauer:
That the life-force is identical with the will.
A rather abstract notion, you will agree,
But it does impinge on our predicament.
You see, I truly have compelled myself so far
To resist my impulse, steel my will
Against attempting to confront you in person.
But every time I tussle with the notion,
I feel this special energy that comes from you,
An *emanation*, and I cannot stop myself
Succumbing to its glorious alchemy.
And that is the *message* of the life-force—
Your presence and my wanting are the same,
They are identical, and they want to merge.

[vi]

I followed you today to where you work
(Oh, please do not dismiss me as a 'stalker'):
I followed you right up to the entrance—
I can well *imagine* you as a librarian!
(It feels so right, you among all those books.)
I wondered should I scrawl a cryptic note,
Or wait for you to come out at lunchtime?
But in the end I abandoned both options—
As I have said, I refuse to disconcert you.
There is a point in the *Ethics* of Aristotle
Where he talks of pleasure and pain,
And of courage—which, he argues, implies
A pain is present, therefore courage
Is 'correctly praised'. Well, there *is* a pain
In knowing (and a pleasure too) how easily
I could accost you, if I dared; but courage
Bids me to expel the thought. And yet,
That very courage (so laudable and true,
And so 'correct') serves only to increase
The pain I feel, the pain of being alone—
Not in an existential sense, just without *you*.
And so I force myself to concentrate
On remoter satisfactions, like these notes
I send to you each day. Please understand.

[vii]

I do not know what you know about Plato,
What he says about women and men—
How originally, countless aeons ago,
The two were fused together, but then,
For some odd reason, some obliquity
Incomprehensible or lost in antiquity,
Were sundered in two, like an orange?
(And you know nothing rhymes with orange!)
Well, since I saw you I am that way too—
Rhymeless and sundered, without you.

[viii]

Perhaps you wonder why I choose to speak
So much about the philosophers? You see,
I admire knowledge, the power of thought—
And philosophy, to me, encapsulates
The human mind at its most empowered.
Yesterday I borrowed the Dent edition
Of the *Pensées* (Pascal) from the very place
I had observed you enter. (Do not fret,
I was discreet—though I never spotted you.)
But here is a quote my eyes alighted on
The instant I opened the book: 'We are full'
(Referring to philosophers) 'of things
That hurl us out of ourselves.' Yes, bravo!
Or as Goethe writes: 'A right answer
Is like a loving kiss.' I rest my case.

[ix]

I must confess I fantasize sometimes:
I lie awake imagining you here,
I probe our midnight privacies and I pretend—
That is the way I am thinking of us now.
I am forever struggling to *envisage* you,
I wish you knew how much I … *cherish* you
(There is no other way that I can say this).
I would dance on a tightrope to—
Forgive me, I have told you too much!
But 'tightrope' is uncannily appropriate.
I am reminded of The Great Altomondi
(A trapeze artist—have you heard of him?)
Who longed for the ultimate encounter
—An instant of utter understanding—
And on the night he plummeted to his death
Before a thousand horrified spectators,
He struck the sawdust with a smile on his lips
And whispered *Yes, oh yes!* as he died.

[x]

I guarantee that you would never guess
The piece of music I have always placed
Among my very favourites. Just a hint:
It is a song cycle, the first of its kind,
Composed centuries ago by the grandest
Philosopher of all, in my opinion.
And the text is by a young Jewish poet
Whose name I never heard and have
Forgotten. And while I have scant patience
For most poetry, *his* words have stamped
Their imprint on my soul. I would love
To share them with you, but am afraid.

[xi]

I am haunted by a comment of Mahler—
His triple jeopardy in three incarnations:
A Bohemian (he said) among Austrians,
An Austrian among Germans, and a Jew
Among, yes, all the nations!
You may not know your European history,
But his meaning should be crystal clear.
Well, I feel rather that way myself—
Not because I am Bohemian, or Austrian,
And as far as I can tell I am not a Jew,
But everything I believe in convinces me
That my categorical imperative is you.

[xii]

Are *you* Jewish, by the way? Do you recall
Those scenes in *Cabaret* where the emcee
Is welcoming patrons to his establishment,
And we feel a simultaneous revulsion
And adoration for his decadent demeanour,
With its lewd choreography and (most of all)
The darkness and chaos we know are lurking
In every nook of that benighted cellar,
Let alone the fate awaiting Europe?
You might ask why I mention this.
Well, just lately Spinoza has me wondering:
He says, in that other monumental *Ethics*,
That pain can be a *good* when it restrains
An illicit pleasure. (Indeed!—you see,
We *feed* on the pain of our revulsion
As we curb the forbidden pleasure
Of an involuntary dalliance with evil,
And this in turn affords us the pleasure
Of the pain of righteousness—a circularity
More profound than Aristotle's equation.)
… And all these knots simply to remind you
Of the irresolvable riddle of my dilemma,
The competing impulses within me:
To reveal myself, undaunted, in the flesh
Or adhere to my self-enforced quarantine.

[xiii]

We almost met today, you do not know it.
It felt like Florence, can you guess why?
And can you grasp how I must tiptoe
Round your privacy, when it so pains me
To distance from myself that sacred moment
When we *should* meet at last? … Afterwards
I kept dwelling on that poignant stanza
From *Inferno*: There can be no worse pain
Than to look back, in times of wretchedness,
To happy times (or words to that effect).
And then, of course, follows Francesca's tale—
How an antique legend innocently shared,
A *story*, that they *read*, alone together
('We thought no harm,' she sees fit to plead),
Brought on a rapture, ineluctable, and then
An ecstasy that landed them—Below!
I cite this not because I arrogate
Such epic measures to *our* situation;
Merely to note that we, too, share a 'text'—
A plot slowly unfolding, so to speak.
And though I am obliged to add
That I detest all churchly rhetoric
Of hellfire and damnation, and thus recoil
From Dante's deathless hierarchy of sin
(Much as I praise his grand poetic art),
You should believe I do believe in Hell:
Hell is the place I am when I tell myself
That I might never share eternity with you;
And if perchance those savage infernal fires
That have so haunted children of belief
Really exist, then I would consign myself
To flame for evermore
If *you* could be there, burning by my side.

[xiv]

You must forgive the passionate excesses
Of yesterday's missive—I was carried away
By what I had been reading. But suffice to say
(I cannot take it back), perhaps it gave you
A glimpse of the limbo that is my lot,
And maybe (dare I hope) it touched your heart?

[xv]

I always found Berkeley a bit annoying
And today he has been preying on my mind.
I mean, I have reached the point, now,
Where I honestly would need you to respond.
These notes I have been sending, unilateral,
Are all very fine but, well, you know …
A time arrives when one must face the fact
Of having serenaded a façade of stone.
The good bishop reckoned that when we look
At (for example) a tree, then turn away,
Tree disappears—it simply is not there,
Except when we are looking! Well, I fear
You lately have become that vanishing tree:
I am beginning to ask if you exist
When I cannot actually see you, and it seems
That lately I have seen you less and less.
(Are you avoiding me? I dare not think so.)
And I must emphasize: I really need you
To exist for me *all* the time.

[xvi]

Wittgenstein has really set me thinking—
On the limits of language and the world.
I have tried hard to make my meaning clear,
To be explicit *and* speak between the lines
So you would know: *This is the way things are.*
Yet you remain unmoved—I am afraid
That I have failed, you have not answered me,
And I must now refigure where we stand:
Should I abandon every hope, enter the Hell
Of being without you till the end of days,
Or must I bring my simmer to the boil
And (contra my pledge never to trouble you)
Confront this demon of my helplessness
And by opposing, end it (forgive this turn)—
Yet thereby risk your loss? A forfeit
Just the thought of which hurtles me
Into such spirals of despondency
As are impossible to speak of.
(Do you begin to see?)
But I am resolved at least upon this:
That which I cannot speak of, I must not
Pass over in silence.

[xvii]

You will never guess what I am about to do!
I have made my choice, I must revise my vow
Not to approach you without permission.
I have no other option—my time is short
And shortly we *will* meet. You need not doubt
Or disbelieve, you need not speculate
Where and when it will be, just rest assured
That in the days to come our paths *will* cross,
And you will see my face, and I will speak.
You may well be surprised
By the way I look, you may well try
To brush aside my heartfelt overture,
Resist my fond entreaties, tell me to go—
I pray that you do not.
But if I fail to make you understand,
You will demand in vain that I should leave—
Alas, that cannot be, or not until
Our predetermined destiny is fulfilled.
For once it is, we two will leave *together*,
Our life made whole again, our union sealed,
Our thankless days on earth (admit it) done …

So now you know—and now I must confess
A slight untruth I let myself install
Into the lines above. As you read this,
I stand outside your door. Soon I will knock—
No need to open it. I have no need of keys.

Notes

Four Last Things

The epigraph (in German, '*es dunkelt schon die Luft*,' here translated by William Mann) is from Joseph von Eichendorff's poem 'Im Abendrot' ('At Sunset'), one of the poems set by Richard Strauss for his *Four Last Songs*.

The Dream

The decision to translate several sonnets of Jorge Luis Borges was triggered by my discovery of *The Sonnets* (Penguin Books, 2010), the dual-language complete edition, with English versions by a dozen poets and translators. 'The Dream', my only Borges translation included here, was translated in that volume by Alastair Reid.

Sour Wine

The stanzas of this poem follow, in structure, metre and rhyme, the manner of a Pindaric ode, of the type originating in England in the seventeenth century. Arguably its best-known albeit irregular example is Wordsworth's 'Intimations of Immortality'.

After Jacqmin

The epigraph is from a book of poems, *Le Livre de la neige* (1990), by Belgian poet François Jacqmin (1929–1992), as translated by Philip Mosley.

Stylite

Simeon Stylites, or Symeon the Stylite (*c.*390–459), was a Syriac ascetic saint famous for living, day and night for 37 years, on a small platform atop a 15-metre-high column near Aleppo in present-day Syria. His cognomen comes from the Greek στῦλος (pillar).

Passarola

Bartolomeu Lourenço de Gusmão was a priest and inventor. He was born in 1685 in Brazil, then a Portuguese colony, and as a young man embarked for Lisbon. There, in 1709, he successfully demonstrated that a lighter-than-air object could take flight—long before the more famous hot-air balloon flights achieved by the Montgolfier brothers in 1783. His device became known as *Passarola*, from the Portuguese *pássaro* (bird).

Non-Incident at the Vienna Opera

Hitler actually was in the audience on 8 May 1906, when Gustav Mahler, director of the Vienna Court Opera, conducted a performance of *Tristan und Isolde*. See (among other sources) Norman Lebrecht, *Why Mahler?: How One Man and Ten Symphonies Changed the World* (Faber and Faber, London, 2010, p.143).

For Length of Days

This *canzone* ('song' in Italian) is modelled on a Renaissance lyric form structured around five end-words whose frequent recurrence across the poem's five 12-line stanzas and 5-line envoi is orchestrated according to predetermined rules.

Inferno, *Canto I*

Other English translations of Dante's *Inferno* consulted in the course of preparing my version of this Canto include those of Ciaran Carson, Henry Francis Cary, John Ciardi, Anthony Esolen, Mark Musa, Charles Eliot Norton and Dorothy Sayers. Editions of the Italian text I relied upon are *The Inferno of Dante Alighieri* (with translation by Thomas Okey and Bolton King, J. M. Dent & Sons Ltd, 1958); *Inferno*, volume I of *The Divine Comedy of Dante Alighiery* (with translation by John D. Sinclair, Oxford University Press, 1961); and Anthony Esolen's parallel text edition (Modern Library, 2005).

Acknowledgments

Many of the poems in this collection have been published previously, some of them in slightly different form. Acknowledgment is gratefully made to the following journals and anthologies:

Australian Poetry Journal, Axon, Canberra Times, Contrappasso, Cordite, Island, Live Encounters, Mascara, Plumwood Mountain, SF Commentary, St Mark's Review, Stockholm Review of Literature, Struga Poetry Evenings, Unfurl, Weekend Australian, World Poetry; Poems 2013 (ed. Jessica Friedmann, Dennis Haskell and Chris Wallace-Crabbe, Australian Poetry Ltd, 2013); *Australian Poetry Members Anthology* (ed. Lucy Dougan and Martin Langford, 2014); *Dazzled* (University of Canberra Vice-Chancellor's International Poetry Prize anthology, ed. Owen Bullock, Axon Elements, 2014); *The Best Australian Poems 2014* (ed. Geoff Page) and *2016* (ed. Sarah Holland-Batt), both published by Black Inc.; *Australian Poetry Anthology* 2015 (ed. Sarah Holland-Batt and Brook Emery), 2016 (ed. Lisa Gorton and Toby Fitch) and 2020 (ed. Sara Saleh and Melinda Smith); *Prayers of a Secular World* (ed. Jordie Albiston and Kevin Brophy, Inkerman & Blunt, 2015); *The Intimacy of Strangers* (ed. Philip Porter and Andy Kissane, Pret a Porter, 2018); *To End All Wars* (ed. Dael Allison, Anna Couani, Kit Kelen and Les Wicks, Puncher & Wattmann, 2018); *The Sky Falls Down: An anthology of loss* (ed. Terry Whitebeach and Gina Mercer, Ginninderra Press, 2019); *Measures of Truth* (Newcastle Poetry Prize Anthology, Hunter Writers Centre and University of Newcastle, 2020).

'The Light We Convert' was commended in the Newcastle Poetry Prize, 2020. 'For Length of Days' was runner-up in the Gwen Harwood Poetry Prize, 2014. 'Compulsion' was awarded third prize in the MPU International Poetry Competition, 2013.

* * *

I would like to express my appreciation to friends and colleagues who contributed thoughtful responses to some of the poems in this book, among them Jordie Albiston, Peter Boyle, Edward Caruso, Jennifer Compton, Andrew Firestone, Richard Freadman, John Gatt-Rutter, Andrea Goldsmith, Sarah Myles, Tony Page, Robyn Rowland, Philip Salom and Jakob Ziguras. Particular thanks to Michelle Borzi, Susan Fealy and Andy Kissane, who kindly read the manuscript and offered valued critical insights and suggestions; to Judith Beveridge and Paul Hetherington for permission to quote from their reviews; to Anna Rosner Blay for her expertise and patience in setting and fine-tuning the text design; to Miranda Douglas for her striking cover design; and of course to David Musgrave, publisher at Puncher & Wattmann.